Believe
in the
Blood

*How the Blood of Christ
Healed Me of Cancer*

Serena Langston

WestBow
P R E S S
A DIVISION OF THOMAS NELSON

WestBow Press books may be ordered through booksellers or by contacting:

WestBow Press
A Division of Thomas Nelson
1663 Liberty Drive
Bloomington, IN 47403
www.westbowpress.com
1-(866) 928-1240

All Scriptural references are from the New King James Version of the Bible.

ISBN: 978-1-4497-8691-5 (sc)

Library of Congress Control Number: 2013903851

Printed in the United States of America

WestBow Press rev. date: 4/25/2013

To my husband, Kyle, and my son, Dawson; my love for you made me fight for my life. I love you so much and feel so blessed to be your wife and mommy.

TABLE OF CONTENTS

INTRODUCTION

I AM WRITING THIS book to share my story so that others can become aware of the power of the Blood of Christ and be healed too! I am a wife and mother who was diagnosed with colon cancer in 2010 at the age of thirty-three, and precious Jesus healed me of it. I do not dwell on what happened to me; instead, I dwell on the fact that Jesus healed me and has given me abundant life now and forever according to John 10:10: Jesus has come so that we "may have life" and that we may "have it more abundantly." I walk in divine health now and I want to tell others how they can walk in divine health too! This book is a word for word, step by step recollection of how Jesus healed me. I was healed from cancer by His stripes and I hope that others read this book and believe in their own miracle so they can receive their healing too! I thank Jesus for healing me and know that He wants to and will heal all who believe. Mark 11:24 says, "whatever things you ask when you pray, believe that you receive them, and you will have them."

CHAPTER 1

Believe in the Blood

I AM THIRTY-FOUR YEARS old now at the time I am writing this chapter. I was thirty-three when I was attacked by the enemy and Jesus won the victory for me. I was diagnosed with colon cancer in the spring of 2010 and precious Jesus healed me of it by the stripes He bore on the way to Calvary (Isaiah 53:5, 1 Peter 2:24). For Jesus' glory I will tell you what I went through to be able to then tell you how He brought me out of it.

For anyone who is reading this and needing a miracle, my heart goes out to you for the fight you are in. Don't give up! My heart is also happy for you that you are reading this and are going to see that Jesus wants to give you your miracle! He is doing miracles today just as He did two thousand years ago: "Jesus Christ is the same yesterday, today, and forever" (Hebrews 13:8). I am telling my story for YOU to hear, so that Jesus' glory can be revealed in the miracle He did for me! So that you can see that Jesus heals when we believe Scripturally, "that believing you may have life in His name" and that you do not have to accept any disease in your body because the Blood of Christ was spilt for you to be healthy (John 20:31). Isaiah 53:5 says, "by His stripes we are healed." In the New Testament, I Peter 2:24 restates that truth by saying Jesus "bore our sins in His own body on the tree... by whose stripes you were healed." Take God for His Word. The Word of God is the truth, "Your word is truth" and the "truth shall make you free" (John 17:17, John 8:32). The Scriptures are the truth and are the way to the blessed pathway to freedom from disease, worry, struggles, and anything you believe them for. Believe in the Blood of Christ because it is the way to abundant life. John 10:10 says Jesus has come "that they may have life, and that they may have it more abundantly." Precious Jesus did all that for us: "and I lay down My life for the sheep" (John 10:15).

Abundant life! That is why I am so excited for you to read this book. Jesus saved my life and I will spend the rest of my "abundant" life telling everyone what He did for me, to give Him the Glory and so that others can be healed too. Believe in the Blood. It was the price that was paid for my healing: "For you were bought at a price; therefore glorify God in your body and in your spirit, which are God's" (I Corinthians 6:20). Thank You, Jesus, for the stripes You bore for my healing. I pray anyone reading this book that needs a miracle will walk away with divine health.

If you will believe the Scriptures "nothing will be impossible for you" (Matthew 17:20). If you can believe one single healing Scripture that God has given us then you can believe in your healing: "He sent His Word and healed them" (Psalm 107:20). Every Scripture is God-breathed. The Bible is the Word of God. So since the Bible says we are healed by His stripes then we are: "But He was wounded for our transgressions, He was bruised for our iniquities; The chastisement for our peace was upon Him, And by His stripes we are healed" (Isaiah 53:5). Just like when Jesus asked Martha right before He raised her brother, Lazarus, from the dead: "And whoever lives and believes in Me shall never die. Do you believe this?" (John 11:26). Do you believe Isaiah 53:5 and 1 Peter 2:24? If you do not believe that Isaiah 53:5 and 1 Peter 2:24 mean physical healing then those verses certainly will not bring you healing. But if you believe and claim the Scriptures then you can have anything you ask for: "Blessed is she who believed, for there will be fulfillment of those things which were told her from the Lord" (Luke 1:45).

The Bible is the Lord's Words to us. Believe in the Blood that Jesus spilt on the way to Calvary. Do not focus on things of this world. Jesus is what is real! Symptoms, lies from the enemy, thoughts and information that is stated as if it were fact, are not real. That is spiritual warfare. That is the battle we must fight. It is hard to overcome in our heads what the world tells us, but we must! Jesus is real! We have to believe the truth, and the truth is what the Bible says. We must fight the enemy and refuse to believe lies; we must only dwell on the power of the Blood of Christ because the Blood is real!

Rest assured and have no fear because the Bible says, "These things I have spoken to you, that in Me you may have peace. In the world you will have tribulation; but be of good cheer, I have overcome the world" (John 16:33). Furthermore, 1 John 5:4 says, "For whatever is born of God overcomes the world. And this is the victory that has overcome the world—our faith." I had to think about that for a minute when I first read those verses back to back. The first verse says that Jesus has overcome the world, and then the second verse says that the victory that has overcome the world is our faith. Our faith in Jesus overcomes the world! Yes! Of course! Because Luke 10:19 says Jesus has given us authority "over all the power of the enemy!" So by the authority given to us by Jesus we can overcome evil in His name! I will discuss this more in a later chapter but I so thankfully praise Jesus for the sacrifice He made on Calvary and for giving us the Scriptures: "For they are life to those who find them, And health to all their flesh" (Proverbs 4:22). Like Jesus told Jairus: "Do not be afraid; only believe" (Luke 8:50).

Let's back-track a little bit so you can get to know me better before I tell you how Jesus saved my life. I grew up in northern Indiana and southern Michigan. I came to know the Lord early in life and grew up in mainly Wesleyan and Baptist churches. I had a fairytale childhood with a mom and dad who are selfless and a brother and sister who are my best friends. I met the love of my life, my husband Kyle, when I was seventeen and it just so happens that the day I am writing this paragraph is the day before our tenth wedding anniversary. How time flies! We have been together since I was seventeen and I still get excited when he walks in a room!

After college I attended medical school for two years and then withdrew to be a stay-at-home wife and mom. We were blessed with our son, Dawson, on June 26, 2005. He is such a gift from God and brings joy to our hearts every day. Now I am a stay-at-home mom and am blessed to be able to homeschool Dawson. You have no idea how happy that makes me to be able to say those words. By the time you read my story I think you will see why I wake up every day so thankful to be a stay-at-home wife and mommy. Some people tell me that they do not think they could homeschool. A little secret is that homeschooling is easier than it sounds, I love it! I think that whatever parents decide is right for their family is wonderful, whether it is traditional school or homeschool. I just cannot voluntarily give up eight hours a day with my son if there is any way for me to stay home with him. I just can't. I think by the time you have read my story you will understand why. I almost lost my time with Dawson. I almost missed the twenty times a day that he stops what he is doing and runs over and gives me a kiss and tells me he loves me. Praise Jesus, He delivered me and I now have abundant time with my husband and son: "With long life I will satisfy him" (Psalm 91:16).

Back in 2006 we lost a daughter who only lived 30 minutes. I was in the hospital for eight weeks. I almost died too the night she was born, from hemorrhaging. I remember seeing Kyle in the hallway, while I was hemorrhaging, right before they put me to sleep and asking God to not let that be the last time I saw him. God answered my prayer and I woke up to Kyle's face above me. I am so sad that our daughter did not live but I am so thankful to be alive for Kyle and Dawson. I deal with that loss by trying not to think about what happened, trying not to picture what could have been with her. I can't allow myself to go there, it is just too overwhelmingly sad. When I do allow myself to think about her, the pain is just as bad as the day it happened. The only thing that gets easier with time is the ability to not allow myself to think about what happened. When those thoughts pop in my head I turn my focus on being thankful that Jesus saved me that night and so thankful for Dawson and that I get to be his mommy. I cannot question what happened because I will never understand it so thinking about it is not good for me. I shared that story with you to lead you up to the year 2010 and let you know that I was living in a very happy, thankful world with my husband and son (as I am now, praise Jesus). I had no idea when that year began that it would be what my father calls "the year our family learned how to pray."

CHAPTER 2

Attacked

I WENT IN FOR a colonoscopy on a Thursday at the end of February 2010 to check on what I was praying was nothing serious. During the colonoscopy they knew they had found something bad. I was completely out for the procedure. I rarely take medicine and so anytime I am given any it has strong effects on me. Although I was under anesthetic I do remember the surgeon saying something scary but I do not remember exactly what was said. I also had to be given extra medication during the procedure, so when I went home that day I was at the lowest of the low spiritually and physically. I came home knowing what they had found and throwing up continuously because of the extra medication (to the point of breaking blood vessels on my chest). I lay in bed thinking "my son CANNOT grow up without me; he cannot wonder where I went." So after a horrific day of emotional and physical illness, lying in the dark in my bed with my family out in the living room, God put it in my head that my mom had friends, a missionary couple that laid hands on people. Praise God for that moment. Thank God for them. The path I was on that night changed and I am alive because of Jesus.

I was a Christian but I had never experienced the laying on of hands before or anything like that. What I did know is that I needed Jesus to save my life. Whatever I needed to do to receive my healing from Jesus, I was willing to do. Whatever you believe you need to do to receive your healing, do it, because healing is there for the taking. Jesus already paid the price with His Blood. Believe in the Blood!

I called my mom into the bedroom and asked her to call her friends, Gerry and Rhonda Thiele, to come to pray over me. Now I had never read James 5:14-15 before, or at least I did not remember reading it, but that night I learned what it says: "Is anyone among you sick? Let him call for the elders of the church, and let them pray over him, anointing him with oil in the name of the Lord. And the prayer of faith will save the sick, and the Lord will raise him up. And if he has committed sins, he will be forgiven" (James 5:14-15). Oh, sweet Words!

I was calling for the elders of the church that night. They came right away, God bless them for that. I was still lying in bed, sick from the medication. When they came in, I told them (in what I am sure was slurred speech because of the anesthetic) what the doctors had thought they found and that I wanted them to pray over me so Jesus would heal me of it. They asked me if I had any grudges against anyone and if so, that I needed to forgive them. Colossians 3:13 says: "if anyone has a complaint against another; even as Christ forgave you, so you also must do." They prayed against any generational curses. They said I should ask forgiveness for my sins. You see, they were not there to make everyone in the room comfortable; they were there so I could get my healing from Jesus. This was serious business, God's business, and may God bless them for obeying by ministering to me. Praise God that Gerry and Rhonda were obedient and not afraid to tell me the truth of how to get my healing.

Gerry and Rhonda ministered James 5:14-15 to me. They prayed over me, laid hands on me, and anointed me with oil in the name of Jesus, while my husband and parents stood around my bed praying in agreement. Matthew 18:19 says, "if two of you agree on earth concerning anything that they ask, it will be done for them by My Father in heaven." Gerry and Rhonda prayed for every cell in my body to be made healthy in Jesus' name. They claimed I would never be sick again in the name of Jesus no more than a sniffle. We partook of the Lord's Supper right there in the bedroom. I was healed by Jesus' stripes according to Isaiah 53:5 and I Peter 2:24. I immediately felt better and sat up for the first time that day since coming home from my colonoscopy and started talking to them. Praise Jesus!

Gerry and Rhonda said things I had never heard

before but would soon become a part of my every-day vocabulary. They said to tell the enemy, Satan, that he cannot cross this Bloodline in front of me because Jesus has paid the price and bled for me and Jesus' Blood is between the enemy and me and I cannot be touched by evil. They said to keep claiming my health in Jesus' name and believe Jesus has healed me because that is what James 5:14-15 says happens when you obey it and the Word of God is true (John 17:17).

Jesus' Blood is everything! Isaiah 53:5 and 1 Peter 2:24 say we are healed by Jesus' stripes. This means that before Jesus died on the cross for our sins so we could go to heaven, He was beaten and striped and bled for our health. See, we have a right to divine health just as we have a right to salvation paid for by the Blood of Christ. In the same way that a person receives salvation by believing that Jesus died on the cross for our sins, a person receives healing by believing Jesus was striped and bled for our complete health. If you have not asked Jesus to be your Savior and have not asked for forgiveness of your sins and you want to know Him and go to heaven, then ask Him now. The Scripture says, "if you confess with your mouth the Lord Jesus and believe in your heart that God has raised Him from the dead, you will be saved" (Romans 10:9). If you need Jesus to heal you, then ask Him now. Jesus says in the Bible, "If you ask anything in My name, I will do it" (John 14:14). The Bible also says, "But if the Spirit of Him who raised Jesus from the dead dwells in you, He who raised Christ from the dead will also give life to your mortal bodies through His Spirit who dwells in you" (Romans 8:11). Then believe Him for what you asked Him for. Now is the time for you to ask yourself... "What do you believe?" From my experience, there is only one answer... "Believe in the Blood."

CHAPTER 3

Spiritual Warfare

THAT SAME NIGHT, Thursday night, Gerry and Rhonda Thiele told me to just keep claiming "I am cancer-free in the name of Jesus" because James 5:14-15 is true and the elders of the church came and anointed me with oil in the name of Jesus, the prayer of faith saved me, the Lord raised me up, and so I was healed. I woke up the next morning, Friday morning, feeling like a different person (INDEED!). My mom, under Gerry and Rhonda's instruction, anointed all the doorways of our house with oil representing the Blood of Christ so that no evil was allowed in. We were not leaving any stone unturned figuratively, or any doorway open literally!

The Thiele's told me how to claim a verse from the Scripture. I did not know what "claiming" a verse meant before, so for any of you out there like me, claiming a verse means you quote that verse and completely believe it is true and claim it for yourself or whoever you are praying for. In the same way as you would claim your purse if someone asked "Who's purse is this?" you claim the Scriptures. If you were at a party and all the purses were setting by the door and someone asked "Who's purse is this?" you would say it was yours; you would take it and you would not allow someone else to take it from you. That is what claiming means. I read Isaiah 53:5 and it said, "by His stripes we are healed" and I said, "Isaiah 53:5 is mine, healing is mine, I've got it, and Satan cannot take it from me because Isaiah 53:5 is the truth and I am claiming it over my life."

My mom gave me a book to read that Friday morning that Gerry and Rhonda had given her maybe a year before. It was called *Divine Healing: God's Recipe for Life and Health*, by Norvel Hayes. Gerry and Rhonda had attended Norvel Hayes' school in Tennessee. I read that book all day Friday and prayed and claimed all the verses of the Bible that it said to claim. It told stories of many people who were healed by Jesus after Norvel Hayes or someone else had prayed for them. These testimonies of Jesus' healing power helped build my belief. That is what I hope this book does for someone else. I hope this book gives someone else belief.

In his book, Norvel Hayes tells people to make certain specific statements after they get ministered to. So I combined all the statements he had told people to claim and compiled a statement for myself. I wrote it in my Bible next to James 5:14-15 and repeated it aloud over and over again. My claim to health reads:

> I am healed because God has already spoken the words in James 5:14-15. His instructions are the truth. I am healed because Gerry and Rhonda obeyed them in my behalf by anointing me with oil in Jesus' name and praying the prayer of faith for me. I am healed, not because Gerry and Rhonda were here, but because I have faith in God's Words! The elders who obey James 5:14-15 in my behalf don't have anything to do with my healing. It is the Scriptures that have healed me. John 17:17 says the Word of God is true, and John 8:32 says the truth shall make you free. Now I will speak my faith. The substance is what I say, but I have to put action to my faith. I will repeat these words: 'I am healed because James 5:14-15 has been ministered to me! I am healed because God's Word says that I am! I am healed because it has been obeyed in my behalf! It is written that when the elders of the church anoint me with oil and pray the prayer of faith God will raise me up. James 5:14-15 has been obeyed in my behalf; therefore, I am healed! I am healed because God's Word says that I am!' My body is healed according to James 5:14-15. James 5:14-15 is mine! James 5:14-15 is true. Jesus is Truth!

(Portions of the above text were derived from what Norvel Hayes tells people to claim in his book, *Divine Healing: God's Recipe for Life and Health* 139-140).

From reading the Bible continuously that day and from remembering what Gerry and Rhonda had said the night before and how they believed, I learned that Matthew 8:17 says that Jesus took my sickness and bore it so I do not have to accept any sickness. I learned that when the Bible says we are healed by His stripes, that means we have a right to divine health. Jesus has already paid the price and all we have to do is believe it and reach out and take it. My whole belief system was opened up. It was like in that twenty-four hour period I learned how to pray to receive my healing and I learned that I was supposed to believe that divine health was my right and every verse in the Bible that told me that Jesus had been striped for my healing was clear as day to me and was the truth revealed. I could not believe that I did not know this for the first thirty-three years of my life. I wish I would have known the truth my whole life but I am so thankful to God for opening my eyes and that I now know the wonderful truth about my divine health.

I thank Gerry and Rhonda for giving me the verses to claim, for telling me what to say and how to believe to receive my healing. They taught me how to believe in the full Gospel. They have taught me the truth about my rights as a child of God and what to do in order to have divine life. I am so thankful for Gerry and Rhonda Thiele's ministry, that they are revealing the truth to anyone that wants to know it, and that Jesus is healing people through their obedience. I am so thankful that they are so rock-solid in their belief in abundant life through Jesus that every time I talk to them they give me more and more confidence and belief in how to pray and claim and what to believe. I always leave them feeling stronger in faith. God bless them for teaching me the truth and showing by example how to have rock-solid faith in it.

Gerry and Rhonda told me that when something attempts to attack a person, they have a split second to decide if they are going to accept it or not. Spiritual warfare requires total belief in the Scriptures. God calls the Scriptures the "sword of the Spirit" (Ephesians 6:17). It is called a sword because the Scripture is our weapon in spiritual warfare. It was not a physical battle I was in, it was a belief battle. I believe Matthew 8:17. I do not accept any sickness in my family in the name of Jesus because Matthew 8:17 says Jesus took our sickness: "He Himself took our infirmities And bore our sicknesses." If you only believed that verse, it would be enough to heal you. That verse is all you need. It inarguably says that Jesus took my sickness! It is past tense! That means He already did it. All I have to do is believe it! Just as sure as He already paid the price for me to go to heaven, He already took my sickness. If all I have to do is believe Jesus died on the cross for my sins in order to go to heaven, then all I have to do is believe He was striped also and took away my sickness in order for me to be healed.

It is now that you must ask yourself, "What do you believe?" That is the only thing that matters. John

3:16 says, "For God so loved the world that He gave His only begotten Son, that whoever BELIEVES in Him should not perish but have everlasting life." Mark 11:24 says, "whatever things you ask when you pray, BELIEVE that you receive them, and you will have them." James 5:14-15 says, "Is anyone among you sick? Let him call for the elders of the church, and let them pray over him, anointing him with oil in the name of the Lord. And the prayer of FAITH will save the sick, and the Lord will raise him up." So from those verses we see that whoever BELIEVES in Him will go to heaven, whatever you BELIEVE you receive when you pray you will have, and the prayer of FAITH saves the sick. Do you get the same feeling I do? God cares a great deal about what we BELIEVE. I would go as far as to say, our life depends on it! Our life depends on Jesus. Our life depends on the Blood of Jesus and if we BELIEVE in it!!!

Let's look a little closer at how important it is to Jesus that we believe in our healing. Did you ever notice how many times Jesus heals someone in the Bible and the Scripture talks about how they believed for their healing? If God puts something in Scripture, it is for a reason. Scripture is the Word of God, and God tells us many times how someone believed they would receive their healing from Jesus before they actually received it. Jesus even ASKED some of the people if they believed in their healing before they received it!

"Go your way; and as you have believed, so let it be done for you"

Matthew 8:5-13 tells how a centurion came to ask Jesus to heal his paralyzed servant and Jesus said to him, "I will come and heal him." The centurion told Jesus that he was not worthy to have Jesus come to his house and asked Jesus to "only speak a word" and he knew his servant would be healed (Matthew 8:8). The centurion's faith was so strong that he knew that Jesus did not even have to come to see his servant. He knew that if Jesus just said the word his servant would be healed. The Bible says Jesus "marveled" at the centurion's faith and said, "I have not found such great faith, not even in Israel" (Matthew 8:10). Oh to have the kind of faith that would make Jesus "marvel"! Amazing! Our Lord marveled at his faith! That is the kind of belief that wins the battle against spiritual warfare! What Jesus says next allows us to see that the reason the servant was healed was because of what the centurion believed. It mattered to Jesus what the centurion believed and it matters to Him what we believe. Jesus said, "as you have believed, so let it be done for you" (Matthew 8:13). I could cry tears of joy at the thought of Jesus looking down and saying to everyone that believes in their healing what He said to the centurion: "as you have believed, so let it be done for you." Thank You, Lord, for the Scriptures!

"According to your faith
let it be to you"

Matthew 9:28-30 tells how Jesus asked the blind men that came to Him to get healed, "Do you believe that I am able to do this?" They answered, "Yes, Lord." Jesus then touched their eyes and said, "According to your faith let it be to you" (Matthew 9:28-30). Wow, can you imagine Jesus asking you if you had faith in Him to heal you? I absolutely can! He did ask me! And I said "YES! I believe Isaiah 53:5 and I am healed by Your stripes now and forever!!! Thank You, Jesus!!!" You can be sure that if Jesus asked it then, He asks it now, even if we can't hear Him because "Jesus Christ is the same yesterday, today, and forever" (Hebrews 13:8).

"Daughter, your faith has made
you well. Go in peace, and be
healed of your affliction"

Another account of Jesus letting us know how important our faith is to our healing is in Matthew when a woman asked Jesus to heal her daughter and He said, "O woman, great is your faith! Let it be to you as you desire" (Matthew 15:28). And then Jesus healed her daughter. Mark 5:25-34 tells another account of how a woman with bleeding for twelve years says, "If only I may touch His clothes, I shall be made well." She touches His garment and is healed.

Jesus says to her, "Daughter, your faith has made you well. Go in peace, and be healed of your affliction" (Mark 5:34). Mark 9:17-29 tells how a man brought his son to Jesus to be healed of a mute spirit and Jesus said to him, "If you can believe, all things are possible to him who believes." In all three of these stories Jesus clearly states that the people received their healing because of their faith in His healing power. These examples show how Jesus refers to the people's belief when telling why they were healed. Interestingly enough, Jesus could have healed them and said nothing, but He chose to tell them they were healed because of what they believed. If Jesus chose to point that out then it must be extremely important!

"Do not be afraid; only believe"

Mark 5:21-43 tells how Jairus believed if Jesus would lay hands on his daughter, that she would live. While Jairus and Jesus were going to Jairus' house, someone comes and tells Jairus that his daughter has died and not to bother Jesus. The Bible says that "As soon as Jesus heard the word that was spoken" He said to Jairus, "Do not be afraid; only believe" (Mark 5:36). Then Jesus only allowed certain people in the room with Him and the little girl, no doubt only people that would believe for the miracle. He took the girl by the hand and said, "Little girl, I say to you, arise" (Mark 5:41). "Immediately the girl arose and walked" (Mark 5:42).

I love this story because I love it when so many wonderful things are wrapped up into one story. First, Jairus came to Jesus believing that his daughter would live if Jesus would lay hands on her. What beautiful faith. Then another wonderful thing happens. Someone tells Jairus that his daughter has died so not to bother Jesus, and did you catch what happens? The Bible says, "As soon as Jesus heard the word that was spoken" He said to Jairus, "Do not be afraid; only believe" (Mark 5:36). I love it! As soon as Jesus heard that unbelieving statement come out of someone's mouth He turns to Jairus and reassures him to not be afraid and just keep BELIEVING! Jesus was telling Jairus not to believe that his daughter was dead! Jesus wants us only to believe in our health and healing, not attacks of the enemy. That was spiritual warfare for Jairus. But Jairus believed Jesus and Jesus won the victory... Jairus' daughter lived! "Death is swallowed up in victory... thanks be to God, who gives us the victory through our Lord Jesus Christ" (1 Corinthians 15:54-56). We might not be able to see Jesus walking next to us when people try to tell us horrible things, but you can be sure that He is there saying, "Do not be afraid; only believe" (Mark 5:36).

"Go your way; your faith has made you well"

Mark 10:46-52 tells how blind Bartimaeus was on the side of the road begging when he heard Jesus was passing by. He cried out, "Jesus, Son of David, have mercy on me" (Mark 10:47). The Bible tells how many people warned him to be quiet but he just cried out to Jesus all the more. Jesus called for Bartimaeus to come to Him. Then they called the blind man, saying to him, "Be of good cheer. Rise, He is calling you" (Mark 10:49-50). Bartimaeus threw aside his garment, rose, and went to Jesus. After asking Bartimaeus "What do you want Me to do for you?" and Bartimaeus answering that he may receive his sight, Jesus said, "Go your way; your faith has made you well" (Mark 10:51-52). Bartimaeus immediately received his sight.

This is another one of those stories that has so many great parts! First, Bartimaeus cried out to Jesus and people told him to be quiet and he refused to be quiet and cried out all the more! That's right! Do not let anyone tell you to be quiet and prevent you from getting your healing! The enemy was trying to get Bartimaeus to be quiet. Bartimaeus was probably wrestling thoughts in his head that were telling him to listen to the people, that he wasn't worth Jesus' time, that he should not bother Jesus. The people telling him to be quiet were not the enemy, but the enemy was using what they were saying to try to prevent Bartimaeus from receiving his healing. The enemy will use anything to try to put doubt and lies in someone's thoughts. Bartimaeus fought the spiritual warfare by crying out even more for Jesus. Then, when Jesus calls for Bartimaeus to come to Him the people say, "Be of good cheer. Rise, He is calling you" (Mark 10:49). I love that because they knew even before he went to Jesus that Jesus calling Bartimaeus over meant he would be healed. That is why they said, "Be of good cheer." Because if Jesus calls you, you know it is going to be GOOD! Then, I love how the story tells how Bartimaeus gets up and throws aside his garment! Yes! Oh, how I imagine all of us would react the same way. If Jesus ever calls us over we would throw down whatever we were doing and run to Him! The last and most important part of this story to me is what Jesus says at the end. Jesus said, "Go your way; your faith has made you well" (Mark 10:51-52). Jesus tells Bartimaeus that it is his faith that has made him well! Bartimaeus' FAITH! I pray we all have unwavering faith like that!

"Go your way; your son lives"

In John 4:46-54, a nobleman asks Jesus to come heal his son who was at the point of death. Jesus said to him, "Go your way; your son lives." Then the

Bible tells that "the man believed the word that Jesus spoke to him" and as he was walking his servants met him and told him, "Your son lives!" The man believed Jesus that his son was healed, and his son lived!

Not only does the Bible tell us that Jesus healed the nobleman's son, the details that are revealed to us should make anyone that reads them completely love how powerful the Words of Christ are. The nobleman asked his servants at what hour his son got better. They told him the hour and he "knew that it was at the same hour" that Jesus had told him "Your son lives" (John 4:53). The same time that Jesus spoke the Words of healing, the little boy was better. Christ did not have to be there to reach out and heal the boy. Our God is so amazing that one spoken Word from Him is all it took! The nobleman believed in the healing power of Jesus and believed his son would live as soon as Jesus said the Words. Well God said the Words in Isaiah 53:5, 1 Peter 2:24, Matthew 8:17, and James 5:14-15 just as He said, "Your son lives." I believe everything He says and thank Him for sending his Word to us so that we can believe what God says in the Scriptures the same way that the nobleman believed Him when He said, "Your son lives." We are healthy because of the power of Jesus' Blood. Jesus' power healed the nobleman's son. Jesus' power healed me! It can heal you too!

"Arise, go your way. Your faith has made you well"

Luke 17:11-19 tells how ten lepers cried out for Jesus to heal them and He did. Only one of those men returned to Jesus and fell at His feet giving thanks. Jesus said to him, "Arise, go your way. Your faith has made you well." Jesus repeatedly says in the Bible, "Your faith has made you well." Our faith in Jesus' healing of us can make us well. We must believe in the healing power of His Blood. I believe Jesus' Blood has healed me now and forever. Jesus' Blood is divine, is supernatural, and is the barrier between sickness and me. Nothing can penetrate the Blood of Christ. The Blood of Christ has been spilt for my healing and nothing can reverse what Jesus has done, "I know that whatever God does, It shall be forever. Nothing can be added to it, And nothing taken from it. God does it, that men should fear before Him" (Ecclesiastes 3:14). Furthermore, Isaiah 43:13 says, "Indeed before the day was, I am He; And there is no one who can deliver out of My hand; I work, and who will reverse it?" God is telling us in those verses that no one can reverse what He does. Healing, redemption, deliverance, salvation... God works and no one can reverse it, Praise Jesus!

Now there are plenty of Scriptures that tell how Jesus healed without the people asking for their healing and the people's belief never being mentioned. So Jesus does heal without the person's faith being a factor. Thank you, Jesus, for having mercy on us and working miracles without us even asking! I guess the purpose of this book is to help equip people so that if their faith is required, then their faith is present!

Let's look at an example of the danger of unbelief and lack of faith. Mark 6:1-6 tells how the people were so unbelieving in Jesus' hometown of Nazareth that "He could do no mighty work there, except that He laid His hands on a few sick people and healed them. And He marveled because of their unbelief." That story tells how the people were so unbelieving in Nazareth that Jesus could only heal a few people. What that tells us is that it is extremely important for us to BELIEVE in our miracles. It says that Jesus marveled at their unbelief. Can you imagine? Jesus came to His hometown and they were so unbelieving for their healing that He could only heal a few people. How sad. They had the ultimate hometown Hero and they would not even believe in Him.

I entitled this chapter spiritual warfare because

that is what I did all that Friday. I fought for my life with the Scripture. The Bible says God's Word is above everything else: "For You have magnified Your word above all Your name" (Psalm 138:2). The enemy cannot stand against God's Word. That is why when Jesus was tempted in the wilderness for forty days He would respond to Satan by saying, "It is written" and quoting Scripture, because the enemy cannot stand against the truth of the Scriptures. The truth is that Jesus has healed me according to James 5:14-15. When I tell Satan why he can't do anything to me I use the words "It is written" and then I quote Scripture.

Spiritual warfare is no joke. It is exhausting and you have to be unwavering, strong, and steadfast in your belief when fighting for your life. That whole day I claimed aloud I was cancer-free in the name of Jesus. I praised Jesus for healing me. I praised Jesus for making me completely healthy. I quoted and claimed Isaiah 53:5, Matthew 8:17, and James 5:14-15, BELIEVING those words are the truth because it is God's Word and so I am completely healthy. I went in the basement for a while so I would not scare my four-year-old son. We tried to not let him know what was going on because I did not want him to hear words like "cancer" or to think something was wrong. I tried to never cry in front of him and never talk about what the doctor had said. What he did see was us praising Jesus, lifting our hands toward heaven to thank our Healer, and claiming our health in Jesus' name: "I will lift up my hands in Your name... And my mouth shall praise You with joyful lips" (Psalm 63:4-5).

Although we tried not to let our son know what was going on, he did catch on to all the talk about Jesus healing me. Well, little kids listen because that night my son came down with pneumonia and he called me into his room and said, "Mommy, put your hand on my throat and pray for Jesus to make it feel better." Bless his heart, he was listening! So I put my hand on his throat and prayed for Jesus to heal him. After a trip to the E.R. for some antibiotic, the next morning he was completely healed, in fact I remember saying to someone, "You never saw a child recover so quickly from pneumonia." That was the first time I had ever laid hands on someone and prayed for them. But it wouldn't be the last!

Let's get back to that Friday night. After claiming my health in the name of Jesus all day long, I went to bed. What happened next makes me want to bow at Jesus' feet forever...

CHAPTER 4

Miracle

I WAS LYING IN bed that Friday night and finally fell asleep. In the middle of the night I was awakened by a feeling I had never felt before. It was a warm tingly sensation that started at my toes and went up to my head, down to my toes, back up to my head again, and then down and out through my toes! Now, before this night, if I would have felt something like that I would have thought something was wrong with my nerves and would have freaked out, to put it bluntly. But I was not afraid because I knew it was Jesus healing me! "He spoke, and it was done" (Psalm 33:9). God had already spoken the words in James 5:14-15, I believed Him for it and claimed them and it was done. Jesus healed every cell in my body. PRAISE JESUS! PRAISE JESUS! PRAISE JESUS! Jesus saved my life! I am here until Jesus comes for me; nothing else can take my life! Jesus has rid me of all disease and sickness. In one of those stripes He bore on the way to Calvary

He bore my cancer in it. He took it from me now and forever because "whatever God does, It shall be forever" and no one can reverse what Jesus does: "I work, and who will reverse it?" (Ecclesiastes 3:14, Isaiah 43:13).

I want to make sure everyone knows that you do not have to feel your healing in order to receive it, that was just a bonus God gave me. Later I will explain more about that feeling and how I figured out why it went up and down my body the way it did. Every word of the Bible is true. Believe it with all your heart. I am healed because the Bible says I am healed by Jesus' stripes (Isaiah 53:5, 1 Peter 2:24). I am healed because the Bible tells me so! The Bible is God's Word and God's Word is the truth: "The word of the Lord is proven; He is a shield to all who trust in Him" (Psalm 18:30).

My throat had been hurting from throwing up on Thursday, so right after I felt my healing, I asked Jesus to lay His hands on my throat and make it well. He told me to lay my own hand on my throat and that I can do it and He gave me that gift. So I laid my hand on my throat and proclaimed in the name of Jesus that my throat be better because I am healed by His stripes and the very next swallow my throat was better! Praise Jesus!

Later, I learned that Mark 16:17-18 says that

"these signs will follow those who believe: In My name they will cast out demons; they will speak with new tongues; they will take up serpents; and if they drink anything deadly, it will by no means hurt them; they will lay hands on the sick, and they will recover." That was the last thing Jesus said before He ascended to heaven as recorded in the book of Mark. If those were among the last words Jesus chose to say I think they are very important! Mark 16:17-18 means that those who believe can do all of those things listed, including laying hands on the sick and when they lay hands on the sick, the sick will recover! Also, Luke 9:1 says that He has given us "power and authority... to cure diseases." Thank You, Jesus, for giving us the authority in Your name to lay hands on the sick and thank You for healing them.

On Saturday morning I woke up and told my husband and my parents (who were camped out in our living room for weeks) that I felt the warm tingly sensation and we went around praising Jesus for healing me. I called Gerry and Rhonda and told them and Rhonda said "It is done" and she told me to now just praise Jesus and thank Jesus for it and give Him the glory. Psalm 33:9 says: "For He spoke, and it was done." She told me to write it all down and to pray to God to let me know how to use it to give Him the glory. So I did and I am looking at my notes from that day right now as I am writing this. She did not know that I love to write. God knew! I pray right now that God's glory will shine through these pages and the power of Christ's Blood is revealed.

I went to church the next day and went in front of the church and told them everything that had happened and that Jesus healed me. The Bible says: "I will give You thanks in the great assembly; I will praise You among many people" (Psalm 35:18). I want to praise His name to as many people as I can and tell of His healing power so that others may be healed. The pastor said I was healed in the name of Jesus and the tingly sensation was the best CAT scan I could ever have! The pastor said I am so healthy that those around me will be healthy and others will come to God because of my story. My prayer is that this book will help others believe in and receive their healing from Jesus too!

CHAPTER 5

Christ Wants Us Healthy

CHRIST WANTS US healthy! No exceptions! That
is something I did not realize until Gerry and
Rhonda Thiele told me and I started reading the
Bible and realizing it for myself. It seems like a
no-brainer. Of course Christ wants us healthy. But
some people do not believe that. Some people I have
talked to think that it is God's will for some people
to be sick. That is why they pray for healing if it
be God's will. Well, people probably are not going
to get healed from prayers like that. The reason
is that they do not believe that it is God's will for
them to be healthy. They do not believe that "by
His stripes we are healed" means physical healing
(Isaiah 53:5). Well, if you do not **believe** it means
that, then you cannot get healed by believing that
verse. Your faith in Isaiah 53:5 and I Peter 2:24
or any other healing verse can release the power of
Christ to heal you. Your faith in God's Word can
only get you your healing if you actually believe

the words and believe they mean physical healing, because they do. Matthew 8:17 says, "He Himself took our infirmities And bore our sicknesses." It doesn't get any clearer than that!

Mark 11:24 says, "whatever things you ask when you pray, believe that you receive them, and you will have them." I am here to tell you that it is not God's will for any to perish according to 2 Peter 3:9. Christ took those stripes to take and bare our sickness and it is up to us to choose to believe what the Bible says. He wants everyone to "prosper... and be in health" (3 John 2). Jesus came so that we may have life and "have it more abundantly" (John 10:10). He promises us long life in Psalm 91. Jesus healed all who came to Him believing.

When Jesus was on earth there was not one person He did not heal who came to Him in faith. He healed every single person that asked Him for healing in the Bible. It does not matter if you are a sinner, because we are all sinners: "for all have sinned and fall short of the glory of God" (Romans 3:23). I am a sinner and not perfect and Jesus healed me. I did ask forgiveness for my sins before He healed me. After Jesus heals the man that could not walk He says, "Sin no more" (John 5:14). Now of course for humans, never sinning again is impossible, but I believe that Jesus wants me to try to glorify God with my thoughts and actions and try to live a righteous life. I will try to be as obedient as humanly possible.

He saved my life and I am a living sacrifice to Him and will try to spend the rest of my life in line with His will for it. The Bible says, "In the way of righteousness is life, And in its pathway there is no death" (Proverbs 12:28). As discussed in Chapter 3, the only time in the Bible when He did not heal very many people was in Nazareth and the Bible tells us He "could do no mighty work there, except that He laid His hands on a few sick people and healed them. And He marveled because of their unbelief" (Mark 6:5-6). He was shocked by their lack of faith! That's why not much healing happened in Nazareth at that time. Oh, if they would have only believed!

As I discussed in Chapter 3, there are many times in the Bible where Jesus says it is the person's faith that is the reason they were healed. For example, in Matthew 9:29 Jesus says to the blind men, "According to your faith let it be to you." In Mark 5:34 Jesus says to the woman, "Daughter, your faith has made you well. Go in peace, and be healed of your affliction." In Matthew 8:13, Jesus says to the centurion, "Go your way; and as you have believed, so let it be done for you." I love those words! I imagine Jesus saying, "As you have believed, Serena, let it be done for you," and He healed me. If someone talks about me I hope they say, "Serena believes God's Word." The most important question in one's life is: do you BELIEVE Christ died for your sins and do you BELIEVE Christ was striped for your healing? What do you BELIEVE? Believe in the power of the Blood of Christ Jesus! It spilled out of His body for you. The least we can do is believe it! We cannot let what Jesus has done be done for nothing. Take what is yours. Claim your divine health that Jesus has already paid the price for. Do not accept anything less. I Corinthians 6:20 says, "For you were bought at a price." My healing was bought at a price. Christ's precious Blood was the price. I believe He healed me at that price; I take it; I claim it; I will not accept anything less. Jesus keeps me healthy. I pray that "As you have believed, so let it be done for you" too (Matthew 8:13).

CHAPTER 6

Call a Lie a Lie

T HAT WHOLE WEEK after my healing I claimed my health in Jesus' name, praised Jesus for my healing, read my Bible, and listened to praise music. My husband, my mom, and I went to the doctor's appointment to hear the biopsy results taken during my colonoscopy. Before we went in we sat in the car and prayed together. I prayed that every patient in that building that day would be healed also. The Bible says pray for others to be healed so "that you may be healed" (James 5:16).

The results of the colonoscopy showed that the biopsies were cancerous and I was told that I had cancer. That would have been the truth if Jesus had not put Himself between cancer and me. Those were just lab results and were dealing with science. Science is of the world though, and Jesus has overcome the world: "In the world you will have tribulation; but be of good cheer, I have overcome the world" (John 16:33). PRAISE JESUS! I had already received my healing. The biopsies were taken before my healing. You will see in chapter 8 how one week after this appointment, we receive medical confirmation that sitting in that office that day I was cancer-free because of Jesus' healing of me. I did not believe the cancer diagnosis though, because I knew Jesus had healed me and I was not going to accept that diagnosis: "that your faith should not be in the wisdom of men but in the power of God" (1 Corinthians 2:5). After giving the scientific diagnosis, the doctor asked me what my favorite Bible verse was because I was clinging to my Bible for dear life (literally) and I said, "Isaiah 53:5, I am healed by Jesus' stripes." Yes! Looking back I just thank God for filling me with His Holy Spirit to respond with the truth! The science was the diagnosis; the truth was what I said; what Jesus is. See, the biopsies were taken before I had Gerry and Rhonda Thiele come and pray over me, before I believed and claimed my healing according to James 5:14-15, before I felt Christ heal me. The biopsies were cancerous. But I did not have any cancer in me anymore and I never will again in the name of Jesus! Praise Jesus that I never had to live with that diagnosis and never will because of Him!

Because colon cancer can spread to the lungs and liver first, I was told that I needed to get tests done. This was scientific information that Satan was going to use to try to get me to doubt my healing.

Why? Because the enemy knows that belief matters: "whatever things you ask when you pray, believe that you receive them, and you will have them" (Mark 11:24).

We went home after the doctor's appointment that day and had a good cry. Even though I knew Jesus healed me, hearing that horrible diagnosis was too overwhelming for anyone to not have a good cry over. We called a top medical facility and they said they could get me in the following week. So I spent a week claiming my health in Jesus' name and repeating constantly that I was cancer-free in Jesus' name. I learned something else vitally important from Gerry and Rhonda. They told me to call Satan a liar. When falsehoods are stated by others, when symptoms try to creep in, when doubt tries to creep in, say "liar!" "Jesus has healed me. It is written that when the elders of the church come and anoint you with oil in the name of Jesus, that the prayer of faith will save the sick and the Lord will raise you up and I had them come and Jesus raised me up and Jesus healed every cell in my body and I am cancer-free in the name of Jesus!" Jesus responded to Satan in the same way when Satan tried to lie to Him. Jesus would always respond with "It is written…" and then He would quote Scripture. In Matthew 4:4 Jesus says, "It is written, Man shall not live by bread alone, but by every word that proceeds from the mouth of God." We should follow Jesus' example. Quote Scripture aloud to fight the enemy.

Tell the enemy he can't take anything from you. This was very important on the ride to the medical facility. It took nine hours to drive there from our house and the whole way Satan tried to put doubt in me. Remember when I said the doctor said colon cancer can spread to your lungs and liver first? Remember how I said Satan was going to use that statement? The whole way to the medical facility Satan tried to put symptoms on me. I would feel like my lungs felt funny and I would say, "You are a liar, Satan! Jesus has healed me. I am cancer-free in Jesus' name." Then my lungs would feel fine. Then my side where my liver is would feel like it hurt and I would have to fight him again and not accept the symptom.

Jesus fought the battle and bled for us. The least we can do is believe it. Do not believe lies. Believe the truth. Whatever is told to you, whatever you feel, only believe the truth. The truth is the Scripture and the Scripture says, "we are healed" by His stripes (Isaiah 53:5, I Peter 2:24). It is my right as a child of God to divine health. I am taking it, claiming it, believing it, in the name of Jesus. I am putting the Blood of Christ over myself and my family and we will never be sick again in the name of Jesus! My prayer is if you are reading this and you need healing that you receive it now and forever in the name of Jesus!

CHAPTER 7

Believe the Scriptures

LET'S TALK ABOUT Luke 10:19. This verse explains why we do not have to accept affliction, why we can tell the enemy he can't do anything to us. Luke 10:19 says that we have authority "over all the power of the enemy" in Jesus' name. That is why I can tell the enemy that he "is not allowed to put cancer in me and that he has to flee in Jesus' name" and he has to listen to me according to Luke 10:19.

That authority did not stop when the disciples left the earth. Jesus continues to give that authority to us, his disciples of present day. That is why the Bible says, "Most assuredly, I say to you, he who believes in Me, the works that I do he will do also; and greater works than these he will do, because I go to My Father" (John 14:12). If you do not believe this then the devil is not going to listen to you. You must believe the Scriptures for them to work for you. If you do not believe that Isaiah 53:5, "by His stripes we are healed," means physical healing then you are certainly not going to get healed by claiming that verse. What do you BELIEVE? Believe in the Blood of Christ! Believe for your healing. Believe you are covered by the Blood for anything you ask for: "If you ask anything in My name, I will do it" (John 14:14).

Believe that Jesus wants you healthy and wants you to have all the desires of your heart: "He shall give you the desires of your heart" (Psalm 37:4). He is just waiting for you to believe you have a right to them and claim them and fight for them: "those who seek the Lord shall not lack any good thing" (Psalm 34:10). "Ask, and you will receive, that your joy may be full" (John 16:24). "May the Lord fulfill all your petitions" (Psalm 20:5). The verse that I repeat day in and day out is John 10:10 and I say, "Jesus has come to give me life and give it to me more abundantly." Jesus came to give us LIFE and give it to us more abundantly! That's why He came! He came to give us abundant LIFE! That is what John 10:10 says and the Bible is the truth.

So since Jesus came to give me abundant life, I am taking it! I am not going to let His suffering be in vain. Thank You, Jesus, for sacrificing and bleeding and dying so I can have abundant life! Thank You! Thank You! Thank You, Jesus! Abundant life is whatever you define abundant life to mean for you. To me abundant life means perfect health, abundant finances, a wonderful marriage, wonderful family relationships, and abundant happiness for me and my family. So that is what I am claiming in the name of Jesus! It is my right as a child of God to have abundant life because Jesus already paid the price according to John 10:10.

You can have whatever are the desires of your heart too, whatever abundant life means to you. Just reach out and take it in the name of Jesus! He has already paid the price with His Blood. What do you BELIEVE? Believe in the Blood of Christ! Believe you have a right to abundant life like the Bible says. The Bible is the Word of God. He did not waste one single word in the Bible. He meant every word and every word is for us. "He sent His word and healed them" (Psalm 107:20). His Word healed me! Thank You, God, for sending Your Son and for sending Your Word! Thank You for Isaiah 53:5, 1 Peter 2:24, Matthew 8:17, and James 5:14-15. The Scriptures have healed me because they are the Word of God and nothing can go against the Word of God: "The words of the Lord are pure words, Like silver tried in a furnace of earth, Purified seven times" (Psalm 12:6).

CHAPTER 8

Victory

T O CONTINUE WITH my story, we were on our way to the medical facility and during the whole trip I kept telling Satan he is a liar and kept thanking Jesus for making me cancer-free. I kept quoting and claiming Isaiah 53:5, Matthew 8:17, and James 5:14-15 in Jesus' name. The first appointment I had at the medical facility was on Thursday, March 4, 2010. It was early in the morning and we were sitting in the waiting room. Remember now, the last doctor appointment I had had was the appointment that I was told I had cancer. What had changed between the time the biopsies were taken and March 4th was that Jesus had healed me, but the doctors didn't know that! So sitting in the waiting room claiming my health, reading my Bible, praying, thanking Jesus, was about as anticipatory as a moment can get!

We were called into the room to meet with the nurse practitioner. She reviewed the biopsy results that the hospital back home had sent her and she said that she would not even call the second polyp cancer! Only Jesus could have done that! Praise Him! I knew Jesus had done it! She said the first polyp showed I had cancer, however, and so I was set up for multiple tests in the next 24 hours to see if it had spread. The tests included: lung x-ray, pelvic CT, abdominal CT, blood work, ultrasound, and colonoscopy. I can almost hear the music to "In Christ Alone" as I remember being slid into the CT scan machine. It was a whirlwind day and I remember with every breath I had to hold for my lung x-rays that I claimed aloud that I was cancer-free in Jesus' name before I took it. The lab techs probably thought I was talking to myself but I did not care! I could not afford to care. My life was at stake.

After all the tests the first day, we went back to our hotel room. Everyone that had come on the trip with me was in the room: my husband, my son, my mother, and my mother-in-law. Up to this point we had no medical confirmation of Jesus' healing yet. I knew Jesus had healed me because James 5:14-15 is true. Getting the medical confirmation is important for Jesus' victory to be known. HERE COMES JESUS' VICTORY!!!

The first test result that came back was my lung x-ray. Remember when I said that on the way to the medical facility that the enemy was trying to lie to me and make me think I had cancer and that it had gone to my lungs? And I had called that lie a lie and claimed my health in Jesus' name. Well, here is where the enemy gets proven to be a liar. GET READY, HERE COMES THE FIRST PROOF OF JESUS' HEALING POWER! The nurse practitioner called my husband's cell phone and he got off the phone and said to me, "You're going to want to stand up because your lung x-rays came back normal!" I jumped up and hugged him and then fell to my knees in front of the chair sobbing from joyous thanks, crying praise to Jesus! Have you ever been so happy you cried? Have you ever had a moment where you got your life back? Have you ever had a moment where someone told you that your little boy would not have to go through life without you? Imagine how happy your tears and voice would be in that moment. That is exactly what that moment was for me. I just sat there on my knees crying (half crying, half laughing from joy) "Thank You, Jesus! Thank You, Jesus!" Everyone in the room was rejoicing. I can imagine Jesus was there rejoicing with us. I knew He had done it! I knew I was completely healthy. I knew all the other tests were going to come back normal too. I knew before that phone call. I knew when James 5:14-15 was ministered to me, but to get the confirmation was like the power of Christ's Blood being revealed! It was victory for Jesus! It was like Jesus was saying to me what He said to the woman in Mark 5:34: "Daughter, your faith has made you well. Go in peace, and be healed of your affliction." The Blood of Christ won the victory over cancer and it was declared that day. Believe in the Blood of Christ!

The next morning I went in for the colonoscopy and ultrasound. I was in the holding area in pre-op, all by myself on the bed, but surrounded by other patients that were waiting to go in also. I remember saying quietly aloud "I am cancer-free in the name of Jesus" and quoting the Scripture and claiming verses in the name of Jesus. Jesus' name is all the authority anyone needs to fight off evil. Jesus' name makes the dead arise and the sick well. I thought to myself, "These other patients probably wonder why I am talking to myself but I don't care."

Then they wheeled me in and put me under. Some people are half awake during colonoscopies but not me. I rarely take medication and when they give me anesthetic it puts me completely out for the entire procedure. In fact it took me four hours to completely wake up in recovery instead of the usual two hours. I do remember them saying one thing during the procedure, like when you are asleep and you hear something in the distance. Someone said, "I wonder if that's where it was?" I wonder if I smiled even though I was under anesthetic.

I finally came out of recovery and they told my husband and my mom that the doctor wanted to see me now instead of waiting until later that day. That was another attack from the enemy trying to get us to doubt and worry. My husband told me he said, "No, she is healthy in the name of Jesus" and he claimed that the fact that they wanted to see me sooner was not because they had found something. Thank You, God, for a husband who fights the enemy for me!

This was the first time someone had actually looked at my colon since I had been healed and we still did not have the results of the CT scans. We went into another monumental appointment room. I was in a wheelchair because I was still half under anesthetic and could not sit up straight and barely could keep my eyes open. The surgeon walked in and she told us that they could not even find the spot where the second polyp had been and in the spot where the first polyp had been there was just a slight ulcer now. PRAISE JESUS! PRAISE JESUS! PRAISE JESUS! His Victory proclaimed! The Blood of Christ healed me! Isaiah 43:18 says, "Do not remember the former things, Nor consider the things of old, Behold, I will do a new thing." Nothing can stand against the Blood of Christ. His Blood was the payment for a lifetime of happiness, for health, for abundant life, for miracles, for protection, and for a doctor to say, "I wonder if that's where it was?"

The doctor continued on and said that my CT scans all came back normal and my organs were all healthy. At that point I said in slurred speech with half open eyes, "Did you just say my CT scans came back normal?" Then I told them, "I want you to know I might not be acting like it because I'm under anesthetic but I'm ecstatic!" Then the surgeon said that along with the normal CT scans and colonoscopy, that the blood work came back normal and my ultrasound showed no inflammation around the lymph nodes or around the tissue where the polyp had been. They could not find any cancer in my entire body! Not only had it not spread, I was cancer-free! Praise Him for complete healing! Jesus, my Healer!

Let me take you to Psalm 21:11-12 for a moment: "They devised a plot which they are not able to perform... You will make ready Your arrows on Your string toward their faces." Exactly! The enemy devised a plot to take my life which they were not able to perform because Jesus healed me and I believed Jesus and not the enemy. The enemy devised a plot and Jesus made ready His arrows at their faces, protecting me. The enemy can never take my life because I am Jesus' and the Blood of Christ runs through me and he cannot ever try to take my life or anyone in my family ever again because I am telling him he can't in Jesus' name and he has to listen to me according to Luke 10:19. The Blood of Christ stands between us and the enemy. The Blood of Christ is non-penetrable by the enemy.

After all the good reports, the surgeon said that she would recommend taking the part out where the cancer had been so that it could not come back and also because taking the section out was the only way to test the tissue and lymph nodes to confirm there was no cancer. Now, I knew there was no cancer and I also knew it would not come back because what Jesus has done is done forever (Ecclesiastes 3:14, Isaiah 43:13). They told me that if they did not take the section out and they had missed one cancer cell in my colon that it could come back and then it could spread and go anywhere it wanted. Since it was the lower colon they would have to give me a colostomy to take the section out. If it had been anywhere further up in the colon they would have just taken the section out and it would have been an easy decision; "yes, of course take it out so I don't have to think about it." No patient would pass up that easy of a precaution. The fact that it would leave me with a colostomy is why she asked me what I wanted to do. When we asked, she told me if it were her, she would take it out.

I knew I was completely cancer-free because Jesus had healed me and I also wanted to use the help Jesus had put in front of me. Perhaps if I left the section in then the devil would be able to put doubt in my head for the rest of my life and torture me with fear of it coming back. Getting rid of the section where it had been eliminated having to think about it anymore and eliminated the emotional torture.

Remember when I said I went to medical school for two years and withdrew to be a stay-at-home wife and mom? My withdrawal letter actually stated: "Having a family and being home with that family at dinner time and Christmas is very important to me" (I love Christmas). And by the way, I really respect doctors and the sacrifice they make to help so many people and the hours they are able to maintain. Medical school and the demanding life of being a doctor just was not for me but I am extremely grateful to all the doctors who are able and willing to be doctors in order to serve others.

So after going to medical school I fully understood why the surgeon was saying if it were her she would take it out. I imagine there have been too many people that have opted not to have a colostomy and it has cost them their life. But that was not the reason I chose to have the surgery. The reason I chose to have it was because I knew Jesus had healed me and He had put me at one of the best medical facilities in the world where the surgeon recommended I have the surgery. If it was just the question of taking the section out I would have said, "of course, yes" but because I would have to have a colostomy in order to take the section out, there was a decision to be made. Anyone faced with that decision has to make the best choice for them. I felt like the only reason I would say "no" is because of pride of not wanting a colostomy, not because it was the right medical decision for me. Well, there was no way in the world that I was letting pride make my son live his life without his mommy. There was no way in the world I was going to let pride take my life. I fought for my life and the Blood of Christ won the victory of making me cancer-free and I was not going to let pride take it from me. So I said, "yes, take it out," so it has no chance of coming back and Satan can't attack me with lies and doubt about it the rest of my life. No chemo, no radiation, precious Jesus took my sickness according to Matthew 8:17: "He Himself took our infirmities And bore our sicknesses."

CHAPTER 9

Choose to be Happy

I REMEMBER AFTER MAKING the decision to have the surgery, which took place three days later (that medical facility does not mess around), I thought to myself, "we are supposed to go to Disney World in ten weeks and if I can just get through the next couple hard weeks of recovery and get to Disney World then I will know that everything will be ok, that I have my abundant life." Being the silly person I am sometimes, that was actually one of the first questions I asked the surgeon after I recovered from the first day out of surgery. I asked if I would be able to go to Disney World in ten weeks. She said "Yes" praise the Lord! I bet you don't have to wait until the end of the book to guess that we did go to Disney and it was Jesus' victory that got me there!

I had the surgery and spent a week in the hospital with lots of horrible memories that are consequences of major surgery. I am not going to dwell on those memories here because they are too painful emotionally but I must take the time to thank my mom. My husband had a cold the week of my surgery so in order to protect me from getting sick, my mom stayed in my room for five nights. I do not think she slept for five days. She reminded me to breathe in my sleep because I would go so long without breathing because of how heavily they had to medicate me for the pain. She tended to my every need. I can imagine she probably wanted to cry those whole five days seeing her daughter like that but instead she sat by my bed and praised Jesus for my health. She read the Bible to me because I could not read due to my vision being blurry from the medications and I was so weak I could barely open my eyes anyways. Any time she left the room to go get something to eat or use the restroom I would have major anxiety. I guess no matter how old we are, sometimes we need a loved one to take care of us. I think it is just something in us that makes us feel like if a loved one is there then everything will be all right because they can take care of everything. Thank you, Mom. You have a gift for being a caregiver and I do not know what I would have done without you!

One of the great memories is when the surgeon came in and said that all the tissue and lymph nodes they had taken out were cancer-free. Praise His Holy name! Jesus healed me wholly and completely. Praise Jesus! The surgeon also told us that a genetic test they did confirmed that I did not have Lynch Syndrome, a genetic disease. Praise Jesus again! The Lord Jesus pulled me through each and every obstacle the week of surgery. Victory was and is His!

The way I deal with those memories and any bad memories is to not allow myself to dwell on them. Whenever scary or sad memories try to enter my thoughts I remind myself how blessed I am that Jesus healed me and I refuse to think about bad memories or sad things. I do not allow the enemy to attack my thoughts either. Sure, there are moments when bad memories creep in that make me sad but I am not going to allow Satan to bring me down because Jesus wants my "joy to be full" (John 16:24). He was chastised for my peace (Isaiah 53:5) and that is exactly how I am going to live — joyfully and peacefully! I choose to be happy. I choose to focus on wonderful memories. I choose to dwell on the fact that Jesus healed me and how grateful I am. I choose to be happy that I am alive and so thankful that I get to be a wife to my husband and a mommy to my son. I tell the devil he is not allowed to make me sad because I have power and authority over evil in Jesus' name according to Luke 9:1 and Luke 10:19 and I am not allowing sadness in me in the name of Jesus. Then I thank Jesus for abundant life, divine life. And then I choose to be happy. That may sound easy, but fighting for your life is work, but work well worth it. Divine, abundant life is worth it and is ours for the taking because of Jesus. Praise Jesus!

This work I am talking about is not physical labor (although it does make you tired), it is all what you believe and the work is fighting the enemy spiritually with the Truth. If you are going through something right now that is turning your world upside down, I encourage you to fight, never relent, keep telling the enemy he is not allowed to take your life in any way and claim your rights in the name of Jesus according to the Scripture. Then rest on the Scriptures.

I have talked a lot about fighting and to be honest it exhausts me just to talk about all that fighting. So let's talk about resting on the Scriptures. This was something I feel I had to learn to do. I would get so tired of fighting and quoting and claiming that I would be exhausted. Then I met with the pastor at our church and he said something that helped my thinking a lot. He told me we rest on the Scriptures. Rest. What a wonderful word, don't you agree? We rest on the Scriptures. So now I claim the Scriptures and fight and then I calmly say, "The Word of God is true and I take You at Your Word, God, and it says we are healed by Jesus' stripes and so we are healthy in Jesus' name. Thank You, Jesus, that we will never be sick again."

At the moment I am writing this chapter my son

has had a cough for two days. I have been praying calmly, "Nope. I do not accept any cough in this house. A cough is a lie from the enemy. My son is healthy because Isaiah 53:5 says he is healed by Jesus' stripes so he is. Thank You, Jesus, that he is healthy and I ask You to take the cough symptom away in the name of Jesus." Be confident in your belief in the Scriptures. Believe in the Blood of Christ. Put the Blood over yourself and your family and rest on the only truth there is, the Scriptures. Psalm 46:10 says, "Be still, and know that I am God."

CHAPTER 10

Going Home Cancer-Free

THERE ARE MANY reasons why my husband is so wonderful but this next story will show you why he is the most amazing husband ever! (By the way, I hope every wife thinks that of her own husband.) Before we left the hospital to go home, the nurse came in to explain how to take care of my colostomy. When she left the room I started to tear up because it was overwhelming at first. Kyle said something that changed everything for me for the rest of my life. He said, "Piece of cake. I got this." Those two sentences changed my world. If it was no big deal to Kyle, then it was no big deal to me. Kyle and Dawson don't care if I have a colostomy; they just want their wife and mommy with them. I am so thankful for divine health in the name of Jesus so that I can be with them on this earth. "The Lord will preserve him and keep him alive, And he will be blessed on the earth" (Psalm 41:2). It is no big deal just like Kyle said. His attitude changed everything for me. Thank you, Kyle, for making something that could have defined my existence, a nonissue in our thoughts and our lives! I cannot count the times through the years when I thought something was a big deal until you swept the worry away with your words. I love you!

After a very difficult surgery week (one I wish no one would ever have to go through) I got to leave the hospital. I stayed in town two more days at the hotel with my family to make sure I was really ok to go home. I was still in pain, under medication, and could not walk or sit well at all. We had brought Dawson with us but had not told him why I was there and tried to not let him see how serious it was. I was at the hotel and probably not looking too good or acting too chipper and lying in bed recovering when my four-year-old son crawled up in bed with me, put his arm around me and said, "Mommy, I don't want you to die." I said (with tears streaming down my face), "Oh, buddy, I'm not going to die." I remember thinking at that moment that I was so thankful to Jesus for healing me, thankful to be rid of the part that had been afflicted and so thankful to be going home to be his mommy and that I was not going to be upset that I had to have a colostomy because I got to live! Yes, I have to live with a colostomy, but the point is, I get to LIVE! Jesus has come to give us LIFE (John 10:10). Praise Jesus! Thank You, Jesus!

The day I got to go home from the hospital I sent out a text message to some of my friends saying I get to go home cancer-free! When I texted those words and looked at them on the screen of my phone I started to cry from happiness. Oh, my precious Savior, thank You!

It took me about eight weeks to be able to walk without pain again. Praise Jesus for bringing me through those eight weeks. And then ten weeks after my surgery (twelve weeks after Jesus healed me) we took that trip to Disney World! It was a celebration in the happiest place on earth! We love Disney, we always have. I could write a book on all the things about Disney World that we love! I remember being there and thinking "He did it," "Jesus did it." He made me healthy and made me be able to go to Disney World cancer-free, normal, healthy, able to walk normal, eat normal, no medications, no remembrance of "former things" (Isaiah 43:18). I rode all the rides, swam, and held hands with my son while we skipped as we stepped out of the car onto Disney property. I had so many reasons to skip; I knew from head to toe I was healthy because of Jesus. "O enemy, destructions are finished forever" (Psalm 9:6). I have my life back because Christ gave His, because He took those beatings for me, for you. Believe in the Blood of Christ Jesus!

CHAPTER 11

Jesus Changed My DNA

BEFORE WE WENT to Disney World I had my post-op appointment. I chose to have the appointment in Michigan so that I did not have to travel back to the hospital where I had the surgery. My post-op surgeon is very thorough and he told me he wanted to do a genetic test. I was so young and to have had colon cancer at such a young age made him want to test for a genetic mutation in the DNA that makes people more susceptible to other cancers. I remember saying, "I do not have that," but I agreed to get the blood test because it would just be more proof of Jesus' healing. I thought I was done with tests like that because they did one at the hospital that showed I did not have Lynch Syndrome, but this was some other rare genetic disease they wanted to test for called MYH Polyposis. So I walked out of that appointment claiming my health in the name of Jesus and repeating again and again that there is no genetic mutation in me because Jesus healed me fully and completely.

Gerry and Rhonda had said the enemy would try to put doubt in my head but to just call him a liar and claim my rights. So that is what I did. That is when it occurred to me. Remember when I had first felt my healing (the warm tingly sensation) go up from my toes to my head, down to my toes, up to my head again, and then down and out my toes? Well, I had heard of other people's healings in books, like if their feet got healed only their feet would get hot (Hayes 140). So I had been just curiously wondering why mine was different. Why did the feeling go through my whole body four times? Why hadn't it just been a feeling in my colon? Just an interesting difference I thought. Well here is one of those times when a reason God sent me to medical school is revealed.

All of sudden it occurs to me! All of these doctors keep talking about these possible genetic mutations. Our DNA is a double helix and is in strands, or lines of genetic information. Damage or mutations to our DNA can cause cancer. Natural repair along the lines of genetic code can happen, but the repair that happened to me was not natural, it was **supernatural!** UP, DOWN, UP, DOWN!!! That warm tingly sensation was Jesus fixing my DNA! Praise Him! Praise Him! Amazing grace.

Supernatural repair is what the body does at the sound of Jesus' name! I love Isaiah 49:16 that says the Lord has my name written on the palm of His hand: "I have inscribed you on the palms of My hands." My body belongs to Christ and it was made whole again by Him. Thank You, Jesus, forever!

Jesus not only healed my colon, He healed every cell in my entire body! I probably cannot even fully comprehend what He did for me. Do you ever imagine what things in life God protects us from without us ever knowing about them? No DNA damage can be in my body or my family in the name of Jesus because we are healed by Jesus' stripes! My body has been touched by Christ. No evil can come against the touch of Christ: "he who has been born of God keeps himself, and the wicked one does not touch him" (1 John 5:18).

The enemy was just trying to ruin my Disney trip with doubt and fear because I had to wait for the results of my test until after we got back. But I would not let him. Jesus has come to give us life and give it to us more abundantly (John 10:10) and I was not going to let him make me doubt anything. I kept repeating during the trip, "Jesus has healed me according to James 5:14-15 and I walk in divine health now and forever in Jesus' name." I would shake my head if doubt tried to creep in and say, "Nope, I am healthy in the name of Jesus."

The results came back and there was no genetic mutation. Praise my Jehovah Rapha! Jesus changed my DNA, every cell in my body was made perfect by the Blood of Jesus. "FROM NOW ON LET NO ONE TROUBLE ME, FOR I BEAR IN MY BODY THE MARKS OF THE LORD JESUS" (Galatians 6:17).

CHAPTER 12

Giving Jesus the Glory

T HE MISSIONARIES, GERRY and Rhonda Thiele, who came to lay hands on me, came out of obedience. They are such great examples to me of being servants for the Lord. God bless them for teaching me how to pray and telling me the truth. If you are blessed to have anointed people in your life, listen carefully to them because "Death and life are in the power of the tongue" (Proverbs 18:21). The Thiele's taught me the Scriptures and the words to fight with.

The Thiele's went on another mission trip to Honduras in the summer of 2010 and they asked me to pray over the oil they were taking there to anoint people with. I was so excited when they asked me to pray over it because I felt honored that God could use me in a ministry. So I prayed over the oil that whoever was anointed with it would be completely healed of their affliction in the name of Jesus. The Thiele's taught me that healing is an actual transferrable gift. The proof of that is in the

Bible in Mark Chapter 5. The lady with the issue of blood heard about Jesus and...

> she came behind Him in the crowd and touched His garment. For she said, 'If only I may touch His clothes, I shall be made well.' Immediately the fountain of her blood was dried up, and she felt in her body that she was healed of the affliction. And Jesus, immediately knowing in Himself that power had gone out of Him, turned around in the crowd and said, 'Who touched My clothes?' (Mark 5:25-30)

The story tells how the "power had gone out of Him" (Mark 5:30). There was actually something that left Him and went into the woman! That something was the healing power of Christ! I am overwhelmed to know that the same thing happened to me. Jesus' healing power went into me from Him the night He healed me! Amazing grace! I will definitely pray over others in Jesus' name if they ask because the Bible says, "Freely you have received, freely give" (Matthew 10:8). They took that oil to Honduras and anointed a lady in the name of Jesus that had a tumor and she went back to the doctor and she was completely healed. The tumor was gone. Now that had nothing to do with me. It was all Jesus. Jesus heals. He can use us in ministry if we will obey Him and believe.

I will do anything He calls me to do. His will for my life is for us to be in health and prosper so I want to obey and do what keeps me in line with His will for my life (3 John 2). He saved my life and now I am a living sacrifice for Him. It has never been more important to me as it is now to support missions and people like the Thiele's so that more people can be healed by Jesus. Now I use oil myself and anoint my family with it in the name of Jesus out of obedience. I will do anything God wants me to do to keep blessings upon us. If you would have told me three years ago that I would be doing that I would have been uncomfortable talking about it. Praise Jesus for opening my heart to all He provided and made available for us.

Gerry and Rhonda told me to keep glorifying Jesus and praising Him so I keep my healing now and forever. The Blood of Jesus runs in me and the devil cannot go against Scriptures. As I am writing this chapter it has been over a year since my healing. In the past year I have tried to tell anyone that would listen how Jesus healed me. If cashiers said more than "Hello" to me I would try to tell them that Jesus healed me of cancer. Almost every nurse or doctor that has seen me has heard me say, "Praise Jesus." Strangers, relatives, acquaintances, anybody that I could tell, I did. I feel like the least that I can do for Jesus is to glorify His name for what He did for me. The Bible says, "Call upon Me in the day of trouble; I will deliver you, and you shall glorify Me" (Psalm

50:15). He saved my life and I will give Him the praise for the rest of my long abundant life! I want to tell as many people as I can so that others can hear how Jesus healed me and they can believe that Jesus can heal them too.

CHAPTER 13

Spring 2011 — One Year Later

ONE YEAR LATER, in the spring of 2011, I had all of my one-year exams. Those exams included colonoscopy, blood work, and lung x-ray. For a couple months before my colonoscopy I had nausea off and on. It was the enemy trying to put doubt in my head and make me worry before my colonoscopy. I kept saying I did not accept the nausea and that I was healed and am healthy because Jesus healed me according to James 5:14-15 and what Jesus has done is done forever (Isaiah 43:13). Because of other symptoms that were just lies, I actually had ten tests or procedures in a six week period that spring. Talk about emotionally exhausting! Any medical procedure is not fun to have to go through and lying on the bed before my colonoscopy I prayed the end of Luke 10:19 over myself, that "nothing shall by any means hurt me." That Scripture covered me for the procedure so that I would not have any complications from it and it would go smoothly, which it did. I encourage you to use that Scripture any time you need it. That is why God sent His Word, for us to use as our sword: "take up the whole armor of God, that you may be able to withstand in the evil day... take the helmet of salvation, and the sword of the Spirit, which is the word of God" (Ephesians 6:13-17).

I rely on Luke 10:19 frequently for my family and myself and by frequently I mean every day. Luke 10:19 is another of God's promises for us to believe in. If we will believe in Luke 10:19, that nothing shall by any means hurt us, then that is exactly what will happen. Mark 11:24 says, "whatever things you ask when you pray, believe that you receive them and you will have them." There is no room for doubt when you are fighting the enemy for your life, but the great news is that there is no need for doubt. Jesus is "the way, the truth, and the life" and "the truth shall make you free" (John 14:6, 8:32). This means freedom from worry, from sickness, from financial stress, and from less than abundant life. Thank You, Jesus, for paying the price for our abundant life full of happiness, perfect health, more financial resources than we know what to do with, and for salvation (John 16:24, John 10:10, Malachi 3:10, and John 3:16). Those who seek the Lord "shall not lack any good thing" (Psalm 34:10).

All of those ten procedures I had in the spring of 2011, including all of my one-year exams, came back completely normal and cancer-free, praise Jesus for completely healing me now and forever! I walk in divine health now and no cancer can ever penetrate my body ever again in the name of Jesus who is my Healer! The Blood of Jesus is between evil and me: "Because you have made the Lord, who is my refuge, Even the Most High, your dwelling place, No evil shall befall you, Nor shall any plague come near your dwelling" (Psalm 91: 9-10).

I will have future routine tests but all those tests will always just be confirmation of Jesus' healing of me. Jesus has touched my body and now no evil can come near me: "A thousand may fall at your side, And ten thousand at your right hand; But it shall not come near you" (Psalm 91: 7). Nahum 1:9 says, "Affliction will not rise up a second time." Thank You, Jesus.

If you are reading this and you need healing, I encourage you to reach out to Jesus as the lady did in Mark 5:34 and take your divine health that Jesus paid the price for. I am cancer-free because Jesus healed me. My health was bought with a price, the precious Blood of Jesus. Believe in the Blood of Jesus!

CHAPTER 14

Only Accept Abundant Life

WHEN A PERSON is attacked by the enemy that person has a choice to accept the lie or not. Accepting something as truth is like allowing it to be truth. I am speaking very literally. Let's take a lighthearted example. We went to Disney World's Hollywood Studios to the nighttime show "Fantasmic." We had waited in our seats for about an hour and a half, highly anticipating this show because it is one of my son's favorites. Of course I feel like I could say that about everything we do at Disney, but I digress. After waiting for an hour and a half, the announcements started coming on every five minutes saying that they might have to cancel the show due to a storm coming. My son, being the Bible believer that he is, said very loudly so that everyone around us could hear, "The show will not be canceled in the name of Jesus!" He did not accept that announcement and sure enough, the show was not canceled!

If only we all had childlike faith! My son knows the truth and the truth is that abundant life is his according to John 10:10 and if his idea of abundant life includes the show not being canceled then that is what it includes! The same way my son did not accept the announcement, we should not accept anything that is not in line with our abundant life. If an attack comes against you, say aloud, "No, I do not accept that! I bind you, Satan, in the name of Jesus." The Bible says, "whatever you bind on earth will be bound in heaven" (Matthew 18:18). Claim your rights as a child of God. Say, "I have abundant life in the name of Jesus," and then state the truth. For example, we were traveling in our car on a winter day and I have never liked traveling in snow. So every time it started to snow that day I would say, "Jesus has given me authority over all the works of the enemy in His name according to Luke 10:19 and in Jesus' name I command it to stop snowing and it has to because even the winds and the sea obey Him according to Matthew 8:27." This is where knowing your Bible verses comes in handy. The more verses you know, the more weapons you have to fight with.

Only accept abundant life. Know your rights. Know the Scripture so you can claim that abundant life. Put God's glory first. Our life's purpose is Christ revealed. Us having abundant life allows God's glory to shine. His work can be seen. His amazing grace can pour out. His love can be felt. My prayer is that others can see Jesus shine through my life. I hope my life and this book show how Christ heals so others may be healed also. I am so thankful to Jesus for healing me and blessing me with the privilege of being a wife and mommy. I will spend the rest of my long life trying to be the best wife and mommy I can be and telling everyone how Jesus healed me.

Some people might say that it was easy for me to believe in my healing because I felt it or because it happened so quickly. Remember though, I believed before I felt it. Also, there have been times since then that the enemy has tried to put symptoms on me or a member of my family and I had to believe we were healed before the symptoms were gone. God gives life to the dead and "calls those things which do not exist as though they did" (Romans 4:17). We need to do that same thing. No matter how the symptoms seem, just call them a lie from the enemy and believe you are healthy. The lies then have to disappear because your body has to line up with the Scriptures you have quoted over it. Our bodies belong to Christ: "Fear not, for I have redeemed you; I have called you by your name; You are Mine" (Isaiah 43:1).

At the time that I am writing this paragraph we are claiming that my son is healed of his peanut and egg allergies he has had since he was a baby. A pastor prayed over him for Jesus to heal him in front of our church in February. So now we are claiming that he is healed according to Mark 16:17-18: "And these signs will follow those who believe: In My name they will cast out demons; they will speak with new tongues; they will take up serpents; and if they drink anything deadly, it will by no means hurt them; they will lay hands on the sick, and they will recover."

In March, we went to get him tested and it still showed that he was allergic to peanuts and eggs. Well, we do not accept that. Jesus has healed him and the peanut and egg allergies have no choice but to leave his body in the name of Jesus because Jesus already paid the price two thousand years ago. The Bible says, "they will lay hands on the sick, and they will recover" (Mark 16:17-18). It does not say sometimes. It says they WILL RECOVER. Of course until we receive medical confirmation that he is completely healed we still are extremely careful not to allow him around any peanuts or eggs. Medical literature might say that his reaction is too big for him to ever grow out of the peanut allergy and the statistics might say there is a slim chance but I do not care what it looks like or what statistics say because the Bible tells us that God "turns wise men backward, And makes their knowledge foolishness" (Isaiah 44: 25). Ephesians 3:20 says that God "is able to do exceedingly abundantly above all that we ask or think." God is more powerful than any allergy and God can overcome anything with a word. God says, "Do not fear, nor be afraid... Is there a God besides Me? Indeed there is no other Rock; I know not one" (Isaiah 44: 8).

CHAPTER 15

I Know a Hero

HAVE YOU EVER watched a superhero movie? We have a little boy, so we watch a lot of them. With capes, body armor, supernatural powers, impressive suits, superhuman strength, abilities beyond our imaginations, and always an admiring girl waiting to see what they will do next. There are superheroes who spin webs to catch falling damsels in distress. There are superheroes that grow, turn colors, and cover women to protect them from fire. There are superheroes that fly, have x-ray vision, and can turn the world back on its axis so as to bring women they love back to life. There are superheroes that wear armor and fight for freedom. There is only one thing to remember, the superheroes of the movies are not real. Supernatural powers? Superhuman strength? Bringing people back to life? Impossible on this earth some might say? Let's see...

I know a Hero!

Matthew 4:24: "they brought to Him all sick people who were afflicted with various diseases and torments, and those who were demon-possessed, epileptics, and paralytics; and He healed them." (Supernatural healing)

Matthew 8:2-3: A leper came and worshipped Jesus, saying, "Lord, if You are willing, You can make me clean." Jesus put out His hand and touched him, saying, "I am willing; be cleansed." Immediately his leprosy was cleansed. (Supernatural healing)

Matthew 8:13: After the centurion asked Jesus to heal his servant by speaking a word, Jesus said to the centurion, "Go your way; and as you have believed, so let it be done for you." And his servant was healed. (Supernatural healing)

Matthew 8:14-15: "Now when Jesus had come into Peter's house, He saw his wife's mother lying sick with a fever. So He touched her hand, and the fever left her. And she arose and served them." (Supernatural healing)

Matthew 8:16: "When evening had come, they brought to Him many who were demon-possessed. And He cast out the spirits with a word, and healed all who were sick." (Supernatural healing)

Matthew 9:2-7: They brought to Him a paralytic

lying on a bed. When Jesus saw their faith, He said to the paralytic, "Son, be of good cheer; your sins are forgiven you... Arise, take up your bed, and go to your house." He arose and went to his house. (Supernatural healing)

Matthew 9:28-30: Two blind men cried out to Jesus for mercy and He said to them, "Do you believe that I am able to do this?" They said "Yes, Lord." He touched their eyes, saying, "According to your faith let it be to you." Their eyes were then "opened." (Supernatural healing)

Matthew 12:10-13: "And behold, there was a man who had a withered hand." Jesus said to the man, "Stretch out your hand." He stretched it out and "it was restored as whole as the other." (Supernatural healing)

Matthew 12:22: "Then one was brought to Him who was demon-possessed, blind and mute; and He healed him, so that the blind and mute man both spoke and saw." (Supernatural healing)

Matthew 14:16-21: When a multitude gathered He healed their sick and there were only 5 loaves and 2 fish to feed them and Jesus took the 5 loaves and 2 fish and "looking up to heaven, He blessed and broke and gave the loaves to the disciples... Now those who had eaten were about five thousand men, besides women and children." (Supernatural powers)

Matthew 14:22-33: Jesus walks on water. (Supernatural powers)

Matthew 14:35-36: At Gennesaret: "And when the men of that place recognized Him, they sent out into all that surrounding region, brought to Him all who were sick, and begged Him that they might only touch the hem of His garment. And as many as touched it were made perfectly well." (Supernatural healing)

Matthew 15:28: At Tyre and Sidon: Jesus said to the woman that asked Him to heal her daughter, "O woman, great is your faith! Let it be to you as you desire." And her daughter was healed that same hour. (Supernatural healing)

Matthew 15:30: At the Sea of Galilee: "Then great multitudes came to Him, having with them the lame, blind, mute, maimed, and many others; and they laid them down at Jesus' feet, and He healed them." (Supernatural healing)

Matthew 15:32-38: Another multitude following Jesus only had seven loaves of bread and some fish and Jesus "took the seven loaves and the fish and gave thanks, broke them and gave them to His disciples.... those who ate were four thousand men, besides women and children." (Supernatural powers)

Matthew 19:2: He came to the region of Judea beyond the Jordan. "And great multitudes followed

Him, and He healed them there." (Supernatural healing)

Matthew 21:14: He went to Jerusalem. "Then the blind and the lame came to Him in the temple, and He healed them." (Supernatural healing)

Mark 5:6-13: In Gadarenes, Jesus said, "Come out of the man, unclean spirit!" The unclean spirits went out and entered the swine (there were about two thousand); and the herd ran violently down the steep place into the sea, and drowned in the sea. (Supernatural powers)

Mark 5:21-43: Jairus came to Jesus and said, "My little daughter lies at the point of death. Come and lay Your hands on her, that she may be healed, and she will live." As they went to Jairus's house, people came to him and told him his daughter had died. Jesus said to Jairus, "Do not be afraid; only believe." Jesus went to his house and took the child by the hand and said, "Little girl, I say to you, arise." Immediately the girl arose and walked. (Supernaturally brought someone back to life)

Mark 5:25-34: Jesus was walking through a crowd and a woman that had been bleeding for twelve years said, "If only I may touch His clothes, I shall be made well." She touched His garment and immediately the fountain of her blood was dried up and she felt in her body that she was healed.

Jesus said to her, "Daughter, your faith has made you well. Go in peace, and be healed of your affliction." (Supernatural healing)

Mark 6:1-6: In His own hometown of Nazareth the people lacked faith and so Jesus "could do no mighty work there, except that He laid His hands on a few sick people and healed them. And He marveled because of their unbelief." (Supernatural healing)

Mark 6:7-13: Jesus gave His disciples power over unclean spirits and they "cast out many demons, and anointed with oil many who were sick, and healed them." (Supernatural healing)

Mark 7:32-35: There was a man that was deaf and had a speech impediment and Jesus put His fingers in his ears, and spat and touched his tongue and said to him "Be opened" and "Immediately his ears were opened, and the impediment of his tongue was loosed, and he spoke plainly." (Supernatural healing)

Mark 8:22-25: Jesus took a blind man by the hand, spit on his eyes, and put His hands on him. The man could then see somewhat and so Jesus put His hands on his eyes again and the man's vision was restored and he "saw everyone clearly." (Supernatural healing)

Mark 9:17-29: A man brought his mute, epileptic son to Jesus and asked Jesus to cast out the unclean spirit that was afflicting his son. Jesus said, "If you can believe, all things are possible to him who believes" and the father said, "Lord, I believe; help my unbelief!" Jesus commanded and the unclean spirit came out of him. (Supernatural healing)

Mark 10:46-52: In Jericho, blind Bartimaeus cried out saying, "Jesus, Son of David, have mercy on me!" He asked Jesus, "Rabboni, that I may receive my sight." Then Jesus said to him, "Go your way; your faith has made you well." (Supernatural healing)

Luke 7:11-15: In Nain, a dead man was being carried out and his mother, a widow, was crying. Jesus had compassion on her and "touched the open coffin." Jesus said, "Young man, I say to you, arise." The man sat up and spoke. (Supernaturally brought someone back to life)

Luke 13:10-13: Jesus saw a woman who was bent over for eighteen years and said, "Woman, you are loosed from your infirmity." He laid His hands on her and "immediately she was made straight, and glorified God." (Supernatural healing)

Luke 17:11-19: There were ten lepers that called out to Jesus and Jesus said, "Go, show yourselves to the priests." They went and were cleansed. Only one came back to thank Jesus and Jesus said, "Arise, go your way. Your faith has made you well." (Supernatural healing)

Luke 22:49-51: When Jesus was being arrested; the ear was cut off of one of the high priest's servants that had come to arrest Jesus. Jesus "touched his ear and healed him." (Supernatural healing)

John 4:46-53: Near Capernaum, a nobleman asked Jesus to heal his son who was at the point of death. Jesus said, "Go your way; your son lives." The man "believed the word that Jesus spoke to him" and a servant met him and told him "Your son lives!" He asked the servant when his son's fever left him and the servant told him and he "knew that it was at the same hour" in which Jesus had said to him, "your son lives." (Supernatural healing)

John 9:1-7: Jesus spat on the ground and made clay and anointed the eyes of a blind man with the clay and told him to go wash it off. "So he went and washed, and came back seeing." (Supernatural healing)

John 11:1-44: Lazarus died and was buried for four days. Jesus said to Lazarus' sister, "Did I not say to you that if you would believe you would see the glory of God?" Jesus prayed and then said with a loud voice, "Lazarus, come forth!" Lazarus "came out bound hand and foot with graveclothes." (Supernaturally brought someone back to life)

John 21:25: "And there are also many other things that Jesus did, which if they were written one by one, I suppose that even the world itself could not contain the books that would be written."

Now, that's a Hero!!!

There is a Hero that is doing miracles beyond our wildest dreams right here on earth today, and His name is Jesus! Precious Jesus. I love Him so! There are supernatural powers in this world. Jesus has supernatural powers and He uses them to rescue damsels in distress. I am one of them. He healed me of cancer with His Blood. Praise Jesus, my Hero! Psalm 138:7 says, "Though I walk in the midst of trouble, You will revive me; You will stretch out Your hand Against the wrath of my enemies, And Your right hand will save me. The Lord will perfect that which concerns me." Jesus held on to my hand as He slayed my enemies. He perfected that which concerned me. What He has done for me is more miraculous than any movie ever could be. He truly reached down and saved my life! Isaiah 41:13 says, "For I, the Lord your God, will hold your right hand, Saying to you, 'Fear not, I will help you'."

I know a Hero, and I worship Him and thank Him for saving me. I walk in divine health now; no disease can penetrate my body because the Blood of Christ has touched it. Since I received my healing I have had multiple tests or procedures, as I mentioned before, ten just in the spring of 2011, all of which have come back showing complete health. Jesus' power is real and at work on earth and through us. He carries us; He heals us; He protects us, right here today. We may not be able to see Jesus when He is performing the miracles, but we can see the miracles happen. We may not be able to reach out and touch Him, but sometimes we get to feel our healing when He touches us. It was more than two thousand years ago when Jesus performed His first miracle. Two thousand years later He is not tired of doing miracles. I picture Him waiting on the edge of His seat at the right hand of God, ready for us to ask Him to do it again.

There is a Hero who is real, His name is Jesus, and He offers us eternal life if we believe in Him: "For God so loved the world that He gave His only begotten Son, that whoever believes in Him should not perish but have everlasting life" (John 3:16). I encourage you to believe in the real Hero that has already bled and died to save your life. Jesus is my Hero! He has saved my life from cancer and disease. He has died so that I can have eternal life in paradise. He is my Miracle Worker, my Healer, and my Savior. Do not believe what you hear; do not accept attacks; do not believe negative reports. Believe in the Scripture so steadfastly that lies are repelled from your thoughts. "If you have faith… nothing will be impossible for you" (Matthew 17:20). Jesus said, "Did I not say to you that if you would believe you would see the glory of God?" (John 11:40). The Scriptures are God's Words to us: "these are written that you may believe that Jesus is the Christ, the Son of God, and that believing you may have life in His name" (John 20:31). **Believe in the Blood of Christ!**

Spring 2010

Thursday

- Colonoscopy done, biopsy of 2 polyps found.

Thursday Night

- Missionaries come and lay hands on me and minister James 5:14-15 to me.

Friday

- I claimed I was healed in Jesus' name and quoted James 5:14-15 all day.

Friday Night

- I felt Jesus healing me up and down my body.

1 Week Later

- I was told the results of the biopsies showed that the polyps were cancerous and that I had cancer. I was also told I needed tests to see if it had spread.

2 Weeks Later

- I went for the following tests:
    ◊ Lung X-Ray
    ◊ Pelvic CT Scan
    ◊ Abdominal CT Scan
    ◊ Blood CEA Test
    ◊ Colonoscopy
    ◊ Ultrasound
- Test Results:
    ◊ Lung X-Ray – Cancer-Free
    ◊ Pelvic CT Scan – Cancer-Free
    ◊ Abdominal CT Scan – Cancer-Free
    ◊ Blood CEA Test – Normal
    ◊ Colonoscopy – No Cancer Found
    ◊ Ultrasound – No Cancer Found
- Surgery To Remove Where Cancer Had Been
- Results of Surgery:
    ◊ No Cancer in Tissue
    ◊ No Cancer in Lymph Nodes
    ◊ Genetic Disease Test – No Mutation Found

Spring 2011

- One-Year Tests — Cancer-Free

Spring 2012

- Two-Year Tests — Cancer-Free

VERSES I USE DAILY TO FIGHT THE ENEMY

1. Psalm 91: "No evil shall befall you"

2. Isaiah 53:5: "by His stripes we are healed"

3. Luke 10:19: "Behold, I give you the authority to trample on serpents and scorpions, and over all the power of the enemy, and nothing shall by any means hurt you."

4. Matthew 8:17: "He Himself took our infirmities And bore our sicknesses."

5. Luke 9:1: "Then He called His twelve disciples together and gave them power and authority over all demons, and to cure diseases."

6. Matthew 21:21: "if you say to this mountain, 'Be removed and be cast into the sea,' it will be done."

7. Matthew 18:18: "whatever you bind on earth will be bound in heaven"

8. Mark 16:17-18: "And these signs will follow those who believe... they will lay hands on the sick, and they will recover."

9. 3 John 2: "I pray that you may prosper in all things and be in health"

10. John 10:10: "I have come that they may have life, and that they may have it more abundantly."

PRAYER FOR SALVATION

John 3:16: "For God so loved the world that He gave His only begotten Son, that whoever believes in Him should not perish but have everlasting life."

Romans 10:9: "that if you confess with your mouth the Lord Jesus and believe in your heart that God has raised Him from the dead, you will be saved."

Acts 16:31: "Believe on the Lord Jesus Christ, and you will be saved."

If you have not asked Jesus to be your Savior you can pray now:

Dear Father, I believe that Christ died on the cross to take the punishment for my sin and rose from the grave. I ask forgiveness for my sins and ask Jesus to come into my heart and my life and be my Savior. I love You, Lord, and thank You that I am saved and born again and will live with You in heaven for all eternity! In Jesus' name, amen.

PRAYER FOR HEALING

I Peter 2:24: "who Himself bore our sins in His own body, on the tree, that we, having died to sins, might live for righteousness– by whose stripes you were healed."

Isaiah 53:5: "But He was wounded for our transgressions, He was bruised for our iniquities; The chastisement for our peace was upon Him, And by His stripes we are healed."

Matthew 8:17: "He Himself took our infirmities And bore our sicknesses."

Mark 11:24: "Therefore I say to you, whatever things you ask when you pray, believe that you receive them, and you will have them."

John 14:14: "If you ask anything in My name, I will do it."

If you need healing from Jesus you can pray to Him now:

Dear Jesus, I ask You to put Your healing hand upon me and heal me. I believe that whatever I ask You for I will receive. I believe that the Blood of

Christ is between affliction and me. I believe that I am healed by Your stripes and that You bore my sickness according to Matthew 8:17. I do not accept any symptoms in my body because I am Yours and I have a right to divine health as a child of God because Jesus paid the price for my healing. Thank You that Your healing power is in me now and no evil can befall me according to Psalm 91. I thank You that I am healed by Your stripes according to Isaiah 53:5 and that I have divine health now and forever because of You! In Jesus' name, amen.

Then repeat aloud (continuously if you need to) that you are healthy in Jesus' name!

EXAMPLES OF HOW TO FIGHT THE ENEMY

The key is to find a verse to fight with! The Bible says that the Word of God is "the sword of the Spirit" (Ephesians 6:17). God has given us His Word to fight with because He wants us to use it as a sword against the enemy, just like Jesus did in Matthew chapter 4. Find your verse to fight with and stand on the Word of God!

For Health:

If your health is attacked, for simplicities sake let's say you get a sunburn. I would say: "No, I do not accept this sunburn on my body because my body belongs to Christ. According to Luke 10:19, I have authority over all the works of the enemy in Jesus' name and I command this sunburn to leave my body and it will not damage my skin or DNA in any way. I am healed by Jesus' stripes according to Isaiah 53:5 and my body must line up with complete health in the name of Jesus." And then believe that the Blood of Jesus covers you.

For Finances:

If your finances are attacked, for example, say you misplace a thousand dollars and do not see any way to pay your bills. I would say: "No, I do not accept this situation in my finances. My money belongs to God and the Bible says that Jesus came so that we may have life and have it more abundantly according to John 10:10 and being able to pay my bills is part of abundant life. I put the Blood of Jesus over my finances and only accept good things to happen with my money because that is in line with God's will for my life, to be in health and prosper, according to 3 John 2." And then believe that the Blood of Christ covers you.

For Relationships:

If a relationship is strained in your life, for example say there is a misunderstanding between you and a friend. I would say: "Isaiah 53:5 says that Jesus was chastised for my peace and I believe the Bible and I claim my peace in Jesus' name. I claim peace between my friend and me because that is God's will for my life and I claim my rights as a child of God. I pray blessings upon my relationships and pray, dear God, that You fill me with Your Holy Spirit and let my words and actions glorify You when I am talking to my friend." And then believe that Jesus being chastised was the sacrifice that was already paid for your peace, including relationship peace.

My heart aches for anyone reading this that has lost family members. I hope that this book finds its way into the hands of people who need it so they can know what verses to believe in to receive their healing from Jesus. Anyone who is reading this and needs healing, remember what Peter told Aeneas: **"Jesus the Christ heals you"** (Acts 9:34).

Disclaimer: Serena Langston is not responsible for what anyone else believes and is not responsible for anyone else's medical healing.

BIBLIOGRAPHY

Hayes, Norvel. *Divine Healing: God's Recipe For Life & Health*. Tulsa, Oklahoma: Harrison House, Inc., 1995.

Believe in the Blood

For more information or to
contact Serena Langston,
please visit us at
http://www.BelieveintheBlood.com.

Prayer requests welcome.

9 781449 786915